CHANNEL TUNNEL

Editorial: Steve Parker
Design: David West
 Children's Book Design
Illustrator: Simon Bishop
Picture research: Cecilia Weston-Baker

© Aladdin Books Ltd 1990

Created and designed by
N.W. Books Ltd
28 Percy Street
London W1P 9FF

First published in
Great Britain in 1990 by
Franklin Watts
96 Leonard Street
London EC2A 4RH

Printed in Belgium

ISBN 0-7496-0723-8

A CIP catalogue record for this book
is available from the British Library

Contents

ENGINEERS AT WORK

CHANNEL TUNNEL

LIONEL BENDER

GLOUCESTER PRESS
London · New York · Toronto · Sydney

THE TUNNEL

Even before the Battle of Hastings, in 1066, the histories of Britain and France were closely connected. But it was only in 1987 that the two countries signed a treaty to build a "fixed link" between them. Following this, the Anglo-French company, Eurotunnel, was given a 55-year contract to build and operate a tunnel. It runs from near Folkestone in Kent, south-east England, to near Calais, in north-east France.

The Channel Tunnel is bored through the sea bed beneath the 34-kilometre-wide stretch of water between these two countries – the Channel, or la Manche. The Channel Tunnel is also known as the Chunnel (a shortening of Channel Tunnel) and the TransManche Link. It is presenting engineers with many challenges.

The Tunnel consists, in fact, of three tunnels. The smaller central or service tunnel will provide ventilation and access for maintenance and emergency vehicles and people. High-speed inter-city passenger trains, long-distance freight trains, and shuttle freight and tourist trains, will all run through the main tunnels. The Tunnel is due for completion in 1993.

▲ This, the first scheme for a Channel tunnel, was put forward by French engineer Albert Mathieu-Favier in 1802. A French tunnel was started in 1877, and a British one in 1881 and again in 1975, but all three were abandoned.

Outgoing tunnel
This is 7.6 metres in diameter – about the size of a two-storey house. Trains will run through it from London or from the terminal at Cheriton, near Folkestone.

The Channel Tunnel
All three tunnels will be almost 50 kilometres in length, with 38 kilometres below the Channel. The Tunnel will be the largest undersea transport system in the world.

Locomotives
The 130 kph shuttle trains will be driven at both ends by electric locomotives powered from overhead cables.

Passenger shuttles
Tourist shuttle trains will include 14 double-deck and 14 single-deck wagons. The double-deckers will each take 120 cars and the single-deckers about 40 coaches, or cars with caravans or trailers.

Under the sea
The Tunnel will be buried between 17 and 40 metres deep in the sea bed. Mid-way across the Channel, it will be almost 100 metres below sea level.

Cross passage

Service tunnel
This is 4.8 metres in diameter. It contains a roadway and is linked to the main tunnels by cross-passages every 375 metres.

Incoming tunnel
Identical in size to the other main tunnel, this will take trains from Paris and from the shuttle terminal at Coquelles near Calais. Power lines, signalling and communications cables will be fixed to the walls.

THE PLANNING

Eurotunnel had to draw up detailed engineering plans for approval by both governments. These had to show that their system was feasible and would be safe to use; how long and how much money it would take to build; how people, road and rail transport would travel through it; and how the construction would not upset the environment more than was necessary. The result is one of the great engineering feats of the age.

Geologists bored holes into the sea bed and shores to find out the hardness of the rock the tunnel-boring machines would have to work through. Road and rail engineers calculated the optimum size for the tunnels and the layouts for the shuttle terminals. Biologists and conservationists predicted the environmental impact. Building engineers and contractors estimated the number of workers, digging and cutting machines, trucks and tunnel-wall materials needed. They, together with economists and bankers, worked out the likely cost of the project and how it would be funded privately. (Their estimate was £4,900 million but this has been exceeded.)

▲ So that they could foresee some of the construction problems they would have to overcome, Eurotunnel engineers built a 32-metre-long model railway system of the shuttle train terminals. They also made this scale model to show the public how the system would work.

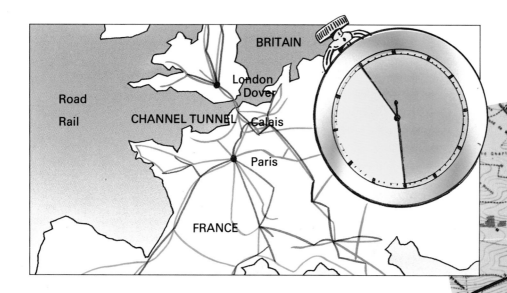

▲ In 1992, Europe becomes a single economic market. People and goods will be able to move freely to and from Britain and the Continent. Currently, London-to-Paris total passenger times are seven hours by ferry, five hours by hovercraft and three hours by plane. With the opening of the Channel Tunnel, inter-city rail journeys from centre to centre will be as fast as by plane.

ALTERNATIVES REJECTED

The British and French governments accepted Eurotunnel's scheme in preference to three other plans. Euroroute consisted of artificial islands about eight kilometres from the British and French coasts, with a road bridge and rail tunnel linking islands and shores. Channel Expressway was a combined road-and-rail tunnel bored through the sea bed.

Eurobridge comprised two giant towers and a suspended tube with four layers of traffic. Problems with the above-ground structures, such as bridges and islands, included whether they would stand up to heavy corrosion by salt water, and resist the battering by strong winds and waves whipped up by the storms that sweep along the Channel.

▼ When choosing a site for the French terminal, engineers looked for flat land on which new railway tracks could be laid easily, close to the Tunnel entrance. The best location was here, at Coquelles, just south of Calais. The coloured areas show how much land the terminals take up.

Artificial islands with a bridge for road traffic

A bored road tunnel with occasional trains

A bridge with suspended shell and four levels of traffic

WHICH ROUTE?

Geologists knew from previous attempts at building a Channel Tunnel, that the shortest undersea route would in fact not be the best. Beneath the Channel lie three main layers of rock: Middle Chalk, Lower Chalk and Gault Clay. But only the lower part of the Lower Chalk is ideal for tunnelling. The other layers consist of rock that is either too brittle and allows too much water to seep into the tunnel, or is too soft and weak to support the weight of the construction.

The route and depth of the Tunnel was planned so that the maximum length would lie within favourable, "bore-friendly" rocks. The result is a winding path with gentle gradients at either end. The gradients will help both the acceleration and braking of trains and the draining of sea water that enters the Tunnel.

Most of the Tunnel's route is bored through Chalk Marl, which is a mixture of clay and chalk. On the French side, though, it will have to pass through layers of chalk that are cracked and leaky. A mixture of cement and clay will be injected into this rock ahead of the tunnel-boring machines, to strengthen it and make it watertight.

A winding route

At their closest points, the coasts of Britain and France are about 34 kilometres apart. The Tunnel, to follow the best route through the sea bed, will be 38 kilometres from coast to coast. On land there will be a total additional 12 kilometres of tunnelling.

The route from above

Bore holes

ENGLAND

Through the Chalk Marl

The three tunnels are being bored through a gently curving layer of chalk from Castle Hill, north of Folkestone, to Beussingue Farm, near Sangatte, north of Calais. Only on the French side is tunnelling having to be carried out through several different sorts of chalk and other layers.

Side view of the route

Geologists use three main survey methods: seismic studies, satellite mapping and boreholes. The first method involves ships dragging explosive devices through the water. Shock waves created by small blasts travel through the water and into the sea bed rocks. The echoes from the different layers of chalk are detected at the surface. The direction and time delay of the echoes provide details of the rock structure. Satellite cameras provide photographs of the area. By boring down into the rock from offshore drill rigs, the depth and hardness of the rock layers are determined.

Satellite mapping

Seismic survey

Drilling for rock samples

FRANCE

A drilling ship boring for samples.

Chalk

Chalk Marl

Three separate tunnels are being bored from both sides of the Channel. The red shaded areas show how far they had progressed by the end of 1989.

Access to the tunnels

At Shakespeare Cliff, tunnelling is undertaken from a platform built behind a new sea wall. When construction work is complete, the giant supply tunnels will be sealed off, but a few small passages will be left open for maintenance and repairs.

Tunnelling to France

The service tunnels were bored almost concurrently with the two main tunnels. Tunnels are being bored at a rate of between about 0.8 and 1.7 metres per hour.

Entrance near Folkestone

The three tunnels will emerge at Castle Hill, eight kilometres from the coastal construction site. The shuttle train terminal at Cheriton is being built close to the entrance.

◀ Breakthrough! In France, on 27 April 1989, the TBM boring underground from Sangatte to Coquelles, finally emerged.

Engineers have planned that the Channel Tunnel should be built from two construction sites and bored in four different directions. From a site at Shakespeare Cliff near Folkestone, tunnelling is working outward towards France and inward towards the entrance at Castle Hill. On the French side, from Sangatte, tunnelling is progressing through the sea bed to a meeting point in mid-Channel and also inland to Coquelles. The central service tunnel is being bored first, to act as a pilot, or test, tunnel.

As the tunnel-boring machines – TBMs for short – move forwards, the ground ahead and to each side is examined. Wherever necessary, cracks in the Chalk Marl are being filled with grout (a mixture of sand, cement and water) in preparation for boring of the main tunnels. On both sides of the Channel, up to five TBMs are being used at the same time.

Tunnelling to England

The French, drilling in the opposite direction through the sea bed, are tunnelling at a slower rate than the English, since they have to contend with more difficult and varied geological conditions. The British and French service tunnels met mid-Channel, late in 1990.

French Tunnel entrance

The service tunnel from the construction site at Sangatte to the entrance at Coquelles has been successfully completed. Boring of the first of the main tunnels is now under way. The French land sections of the Tunnel are only 3.2 kilometres in length.

French construction site

At Sangatte, a giant shaft has been built in the shore. This houses a working platform from which operate the TBMs and the pumps that remove loose rock and earth (spoil) from the cutting face.

BORING FROM ENGLAND

At Shakespeare Cliff the construction site is on two levels, the Upper and Lower. At the Upper Site, on top of the cliff, is an accommodation camp for the 400 or more tunnel workers, and access roads for construction traffic.

The Lower Site comprises a work platform beside the sea (see below) and the underground tunnel-boring and building area, shown here. All personnel and materials enter and leave the tunnel workings through four access tunnels. The supply tunnel leads from a store depot at the surface to the cross-Channel tunnels. Inside it are five special rail tracks along which electric locomotives pull goods wagons from the surface carrying down cables, concrete lining segments and pipes. On their return journeys, they take spoil to the main conveyor, which carries it to the surface for disposal.

From this location, the TBMs are working outwards in two directions: towards Castle Hill and to the mid-Channel meeting point. There is a constant movement of people, materials, spoil and machines.

TO TERMINAL

Supply tunnel

Main conveyor

To the surface
Waste soil and rock are brought to the surface by a long conveyor belt inside one of the sloping access tunnels.

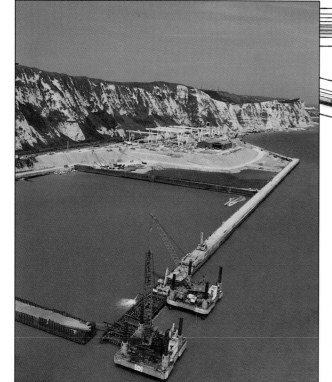

▲ At the Lower Site, the work platform has been built on land created by constructing a new sea wall and filling the space behind it with spoil from the tunnel workings.

Conveyors carrying the spoil.

Personnel access

A 10-metre diameter vertical access tunnel leads from the Upper Site to the underground workings. Tunnellers travel to and from their workplace in lifts, like those in a coal mine.

Lifts

Supply tunnel

From the main supply tunnel, branches of the special electric railway network cross-link and run into the three cross-Channel tunnels. As the TBMs work forwards the rail tracks are extended, to carry materials and spoil to and from the workfaces.

STEEP SLOPES

The slope in the supply tunnel is so steep that ordinary locomotive wheels would constantly slip on the rails – going up as well as down. The locomotives have therefore been fitted with a rack-and-pinion (toothed-wheel and rail) system like the trains that run on steep mountainsides.

Toothed drive gear

Toothed rail

Loaded materials train

Rack locomotive

Spoil conveyor

Spoil conveyor

Empty spoil wagons

Conveying the spoil

Conveyor belts attached to the TBMs load spoil into empty train wagons. The wagons transfer the spoil into bunkers, and from these it is carried to the surface by the main conveyor.

Spoil bunker

Train tipping spoil

Spoil bunker

TBM erection chamber

TO FRANCE

Spoil tipped from wagons

Spoil bunker

Main conveyor to surface

BORING FROM FRANCE

On the French side, a giant access shaft has been built in the shore. Within this the engineers have constructed dozens of tunnel-building and spoil-removal systems.

The shaft is more than 65 metres tall and 56 metres in diameter. Inside, 28.5 metres below ground level, is the main working platform. From here, the TBMs are working inland and out into the sea bed, creating the cross-Channel tunnels. A system of conveyor belts and electric trains leads through the base of the shaft, removing spoil and bringing in construction materials.

At the top of the shaft are overhead cranes used to lower sections of tunnel lining on to the working platform and to help with the installation of the TBMs. Built along one side of the shaft are offices and changing rooms for the shaft workforce, which totals almost 1,800. The workers operate in shifts of 8 to 10 hours, and rarely come to the surface during that time. Within the shaft, food, drink and toilet facilities are all available. All activities in and around the shaft are monitored from a central control room that is filled with TV screens and computers.

Construction and operation of the Sangatte shaft is a remarkable feat of engineering. It is a self-contained building site with its own life-support system for the workforce and emergency services, comprising ambulance and fire-fighting equipment.

▼ To construct the shaft at Sangatte, first the outer perimeter wall was built. Then, using bulldozers, excavators and cranes, the earth inside was removed. Finally, the various platforms and supply systems were installed.

Grout
As soon as sections of tunnel lining are installed, the joints between them are filled with grout. This is made on site and pumped into a giant container in the shaft, through 340 metres of tubing.

Overhead cranes
There are two main crane systems. The largest, with a lifting capacity of 430 tonnes, is used to install the TBMs. The other system can carry loads of up to 60 tonnes. It is used to place tunnel linings in the shaft.

Manriders
Teams of 25 workers at a time travel from the changing rooms alongside the shaft to the worksite lifts in small trains, known as draisines or "manriders".

Batteries
Construction locomotives running in and out of the shaft to the TBMs are battery-powered so that diesel fumes do not fill the workplace. The batteries are regularly changed and recharged.

Lifts
There are a total of five lifts in the shaft: two ordinary, and three heavy-duty. The latter are fitted with train rails so that manriders can drive straight into them and exit directly into the railway system at the base of the shaft.

Spoil from the face
Rock and earth are carried from the workfaces by trains to hoppers. These channel them on to conveyors leading to the crushers.

Tipped into crushers
Spoil is dumped into crushing machines beneath the working platform, where it is mixed with water and pumped out of the shaft.

Tunnel linings
Special flat-trailer wagons are used to carry concrete and iron lining sections to the workfaces, where they are installed mechanically.

A French Tunnel-Boring Machine (TBM)

The Control room of a TBM

The cutting head

The rotating head is fitted with more than 100 cutting rollers and 200 picking "teeth". These are all made of tungsten, a very hard and tough metal also used for armour plating in tanks.

Hydraulic motor

This pushes forwards or retracts the cutting teeth a few centimetres for maximum efficiency.

Steer shoes

Fine adjustment of the TBM's alignment is by means of a series of rams pushed against the walls.

Electric drive motor

A huge electric motor and gear system are used to rotate the cutting head at a variable speed.

TBMs

Like a mole digging through soil, each TBM cuts its way through rock. The largest TBMs, used to build the main tunnels, each measure 8.7 metres in diameter, more than 15 metres in length and 1,300 tonnes in weight. Behind each TBM, in fact, there is a type of train – the construction train. More than 180 metres long and with over 1,000 tonnes of accessories, this contains a conveyor belt system for removing the spoil from the cutting face, and machinery for fitting concrete tunnel-lining segments to the hewn-out rock. It is constantly being moved forward to keep up with the TBM.

The gripper unit

The cutting head is fixed onto this section of the TBM, which is moved forwards by means of four hydraulic rams, and stabilized by gripper pads pushed firmly against the surrounding rock. The control cabin and start of the spoil conveyor are housed here, too.

Conveyor

Push rams

To bore forwards, the cutting head must be pushed hard against the rock. This is the function of the hydraulic (fluid-pressure) push rams.

Computer control

The TBM operator sits in a control cabin equipped with closed-circuit television cameras, guidance system and computerized monitoring equipment.

The TBMs and construction trains were built, a section at a time, at the Shakespeare Cliff and Sangatte sites. Depending on the rock conditions, a TBM cutting head rotates 1.5 to 3 times each minute, and moves forward at about 12 centimetres in that time. For every 1.6 metres of progress, it cuts away 100 cubic metres of rock.

TUNNEL LININGS

As the TBMs work forwards, segments of tunnel lining are fitted to the cut rock. The segments are brought to the workface on flat wagons pushed by electric locomotives (see pages 12-13). The tunnel walls are made up of thousands of lining rings, each composed of several of the segments, each weighing between 3.5 and 8 tonnes.

On the English side, the lining segments are pushed together snugly, and the joints and the gaps between them and the surrounding rock filled with grout. On the French side, where it is necessary to make the lining more watertight, the segments are bolted together and fitted with rubber seals.

▶ Each ring of the tunnel is made up of at least six segments and is constructed in about 15 minutes. With 268 different shapes and sizes of segment, delivery of the correct segments to the right place, at the right time, is a complex task involving elaborate computer systems.

Lower segment erector
Segments forming the floor of each tunnel, on which a roadway or rail track is to be laid, are pushed down by rams.

Upper segment erector
Roof segments are taken from the conveyor belt and forced against the rockface with rams controlled by levers and gears.

Segment conveyor
An overhead crane lifts segments from the storage platform on to the conveyor belt. From here they pass to the erectors.

Altogether more than 700,000 concrete and iron lining segments will be used to build the Channel Tunnel. In England, the segments are being made at a factory on the Isle of Grain, east of London, and transported to Shakespeare Cliff – some 45 kilometres away – by train. In France, they are made at Sangatte, at the same site as the access shaft, and are carried to the supply wagons by mobile cranes. More than 600 people are involved in segment production and transport.

Each concrete tunnel lining segment consists of a curved slab of concrete moulded around a meshwork of metal rods and wire reinforcement. The concrete is hardened in giant heating rooms, a process that takes 6-8 hours. The segments are expected to last for at least 100 years before they are replaced.

18

Making tunnel lining segments

Positioning a tunnel lining segment

Spoil conveyor
This carries loose rock and earth from the TBM cutting head to waiting "muck wagons" further along the train.

Ventilation shaft
Giant ducts conduct fresh air into the work area and carry away vehicle and machinery fumes and spent air.

Segment storage
Segments are stacked on their side or flat, depending on their shape, size and construction. The rate of fitting the segments is matched by an equal rate of their delivery by the supply trains.

Permanent deck
Extending the full length of the construction train is a flat, solid floor along which all the mobile machinery moves. This, too, is made in sections of preformed concrete slabs.

Segment unloader
Lining and permanent deck segments are lifted from the wagons by crane, one at a time.

Segment wagons
About six wagons at a time are used to carry concrete and iron segments to the workface. This is sufficient for two complete rings of the tunnel and the corresponding extension of the permanent deck.

THE TAIL END

There is just as much activity going on at the rear of each TBM construction train, as there is at the front! Every half-hour or so, a pair of locomotives passes through, hauling 20 or more wagons at a time. This train runs on rails fitted to the permanent deck. There are two types of wagon: flat trailers for carrying tunnel-building materials, and open trucks for trains transporting rubble and earth from the cutting head. Each spoil truck can carry about 14 cubic metres – enough to fill an average-sized room of a normal house.

At the end of each work shift, a riding car attached to the front locomotive carries a new team of tunnellers to the site and takes away the tired team. Throughout the day, the spoil conveyor belt brings muck from the TBM and drops it into the waiting empty trucks. And as tunnel-boring progresses, machinery and equipment are extended or dismantled and moved along, to keep pace with the cutting head. These include cranes, erectors, loaders, mechanical arms and hydraulic rams, lighting, ventilation and communications systems.

Throughout the tail end of the construction train – the rear 40 metres shown here – the tunnel lining has been completed and fully grouted and sealed.

Moving conveyor
The spoil conveyor belt is more than 100 metres in length and can carry hundreds of cubic metres of muck in one hour.

Conveyor drive unit
An electric motor and gear system keeps the spoil conveyor belt in constant motion.

Loading spoil
One after the other, empty trucks are moved into position beneath the end of the spoil conveyor.

KEEPING STRAIGHT

Laser beams are used to check that the TBMs follow a straight line through the rock. These light beams are rod-like and spread out very little, even over several kilometres. They are also used like plumb-lines, spirit levels and rulers, to check that construction train machinery is exactly vertical or horizontal. By lining up a number of laser beams, engineers can measure small changes in position, or movements of equipment.

▲ Equipment and tunnellers are brought to the tail end by train wagons which also take back the spoil.

Support systems
The tail end is filled with electric cables for lighting and machinery, and ventilation ducts.

Extending ventilation
From a moving platform, new sections of ventilation duct are added as the construction train moves forwards.

Riding car
Up to 25 tunnellers at a time are transported in a special personnel wagon, to and from the worksite.

Locomotive
The electric locos are only about 6 metres long and 2 metres high but they can pull more than 200 tonnes.

Fresh air supply
Huge air pumps at Folkestone and Sangatte will blow fresh air into the service tunnel. From here it will pass through the cross-passages into the main tunnels. As trains travel through they help the air to move along these tunnels.

Two-way traffic
Trains will usually run in one direction only in each main tunnel. However, there are two cross-over points in the undersea section of the Tunnel, so that single-line working is possible for maintenance, or should a train break down in one tunnel.

Carriages
Tourist shuttles will be up to 28 carriages long. The front carriage is for loading vehicles only. Vehicles are carried on subsequent carriages (shown below). Freight is carried on separate trains.

▲ The Tunnel will be controlled from two operations rooms, one at each terminal. These will monitor train traffic, road traffic, power supplies, heating, lighting and ventilation in the tunnels.

HOW THE TUNNEL WORKS

At all times, conditions within Eurotunnel will be suitable not only for the safe and comfortable transit of train passengers, but also to allow routine inspection and maintenance of the structure and its equipment. An efficient ventilation system will ensure that there is no build-up of fumes.

Locomotives

The electric 130 kph shuttle locomotives will run on the same size (gauge) track as the through trains, but their greater body width and height mean the Shuttles will not be able to travel on the ordinary European rail networks.

Four different types of train will run through Eurotunnel, providing rapid, reliable, round-the-clock transport between Britain and the Continent. At peak times, up to 20 trains each hour will be whistling through in each direction. Most frequent will be the tourist shuttles. These will travel between the terminals at Cheriton and Coquelles and take cars, caravans, coaches, motorcycles, bicycles and their passengers. The journey time will be about 35 minutes. Running less often, and more slowly, will be freight shuttles transporting trucks.

High-speed passenger trains and overnight sleeper trains – up to four each hour – will travel through the Tunnel, on their way between London's proposed new international rail terminal at Waterloo, and major European cities such as Paris, Brussels and Frankfurt. Finally the container-wagon, transporter and bulk-load trains will carry freight between all parts of Britain and mainland Europe. By using the Tunnel, it will be possible to deliver several cartons of this book from a printer in Manchester to a shop in Amsterdam, on the same day.

Air flow

Piston-relief duct

As trains pass through the main tunnels, they push and pressurize the air in front of them. To release this pressure, air vents will be fitted between the train tunnels.

THE TERMINALS

▶ A scale model of the terminal in England shows the complex arrangement of rail lines and platforms.

At both Cheriton and Coquelles terminals, engineers have planned four main areas: toll booths where tickets are purchased; passport and customs control; shops and refreshments; and vehicle loading and unloading platforms. When complete, the English site will cover more than 140 hectares and the French site 700 hectares. (A soccer pitch is about one hectare.)

The terminals are already two of the largest construction sites in Europe. Bridges, access roads, flyovers, railway tracks and platforms are all being built, often using new methods of engineering. Some bridges, for instance, are being planned and built in stages.

▼ A close-up of a scale model of the terminal shows how vehicles will be loaded onto the trains. Vehicles load on at the rear of the train and unload at the front. Freight lorries are loaded onto separate trains from the tourist traffic with special light-weight wagons.

▲ Full-sized models of wagons were made to ensure safe and rapid loading. Above is one of the earlier designs.

▲▶ The interior of a double-deck wagon shows the shutters and access doors that close off each wagon after loading.

Shuttle trains will be made up of several carrier wagons and a locomotive at each end. At the rear will be one or more special loading wagons, and at the front one or more for unloading. On departure, cars and lorries enter the shuttle and drive straight down inside the wagons or sections until they are all full. Then the loading doors shut and the train moves off. At the other end, the vehicles drive off in procession.

▶ Below right is a single-deck loader attached to a locomotive. Above right shows how the segments of the loader door draw back to allow high-sided vehicles to enter the train unhindered.

SAFETY FIRST

The Eurotunnel project incorporates a wide range of safety features. These should ensure that in the event of a rail accident, breakdown or fire, emergency services will be on the scene in minutes, and passengers will reach the open air quickly and with the minimum of risk. There will also be systems to prevent the tunnels being flooded, and to stop wild animals infected with rabies passing through from France to Britain.

Most of the safety features will be located in the service tunnel and its passageways. In the main tunnels there will be a range of surveillance and monitoring equipment. In the case of an emergency, passengers should leave a train and enter the service tunnel. From here they will walk or be taken by coach, or by train in the other main tunnel, to the exit. It is estimated that all passengers – up to 1,500 per train – could be evacuated from the Tunnel well within 90 minutes.

The Tunnel will operate using a number of "back-up" and "fail-safe" systems. Should one control centre shut down, the other automatically takes over. If the power supply from either terminal fails, the other terminal will switch electricity to both halves of the Tunnel. Trains then still run, but more slowly and less often.

Firefighting vehicle
In the event of a fire, fire tenders drive along the roadway in the service tunnel to the cross-passageways. Fire hoses will be connected to a tunnel water-pipe system supplied with fresh water from each shore. Firemen will also use portable extinguishers.

Emergency telephone

Air dampers
Doors leading from the main tunnels into the service tunnel are to be fitted with grilles that allow air to pass through in only one direction. This prevents the "piston effect" on air of passing trains reaching the service tunnel.

Airflow
Air pressure in the service tunnel will be kept at a higher level than in the main tunnels. This aims to ensure good ventilation of the trains and carriages.

Emergency transport
Police, ambulance and fire crews rush to the scene of an accident in special vehicles from each terminal. The emergency crews will be trained to operate the Tunnel's special safety equipment.

CHANGING TRACKS

There are two train cross-over points, roughly one-third of the distance into the Tunnel, under the sea at each end. Should a train break down in the tunnel, passengers will transfer via the service tunnel to the other train. Trains will then run in both directions along one track.

Broken-down train

Cross-over

Train passes

Loudspeakers

Emergency lights

Walkway

Continuously welded rails

Video monitoring

Video cameras constantly survey the tunnels and, with the help of a public address (tannoy) system, direct evacuating passengers to exit routes.

Cooling pipes

Hot-wheel and hot-axle detectors

At each train tunnel entrance and near the cross-over points, there will be detectors indicating when a train's brakes have seized, or its wheels have been derailed. The detectors will send warning signals to the control centre, where an operator will be able to warn the train at the flick of a switch.

▶ Passengers stay in their cars during the shuttle journey. Should a fire break out in a shuttle wagon, automatic fire extinguishers switch on and fire doors seal the wagon from the rest of the train. Fire crews should be on the scene in minutes.

THE YOUNG ENGINEER

Modern tunnelling dates back to the start of the Industrial Revolution in Europe, in the 1700s. Then, tunnels were built to take canals underground. The principles of construction developed by the 18th-century engineers are the same as those now being used to build the Channel Tunnel. Try the projects shown here, which demonstrate some of the basic scientific laws involved in designing and constructing a tunnel. All of these principles are being used in the Channel Tunnel; on a much larger scale! Look back through the book. Can you see where they appear?

Tunnel shapes

Tunnel walls are curved or arched to give greatest strength (page 18). Place a curved sheet of card between two bricks and put bricks on top of the card, one at a time. The weight of the load is evenly distributed and shared between the two curved sides. Now lay a flat sheet of card between two bricks. Again, add bricks one at a time. This time, the load is concentrated in the middle of the card. Compare the strength of the curved and flat "tunnel walls" by adding bricks until each collapses under the strain. Which is strongest? How does a V-shaped wall stand up to loads?

Curved

Weight

Bricks

Weight distribution

Thin card

Flat

Weight

Thin card

Roof collapses

Piston-relief tunnels

As trains move fast through a tunnel, they compress the air in front of them (page 23). To prevent a build-up of air pressure, Eurotunnel has a number of piston-relief tunnels. You can see for yourself how these will allow high-pressure air to escape. Compare the force of air on a feather when you blow – first through a straw with holes cut in it, and second through one without holes. How does the diameter of the straw affect the air flow? Try blowing with wider or narrower straws.

Air blown down straws

Holes cut in straw

Piston-relief tunnel

Drilling holes

There are two ways of boring tunnels. Tunnels in rock are generally made by drilling and blasting with dynamite. Those in soft ground are bored by scraping — and then immediately supporting the walls with lining segments. However the Channel Tunnel, being built through the sea bed, is not being bored using explosives, for fear of water pouring in. And it is too large to drill or scrape out using ordinary tunnelling machines. The rotating cutting heads of the TBMs are fitted with hundreds of cutting rollers and teeth that pick and scrape away at the rock. You can see how effective this is. First, compare the effort needed to chisel and electrically drill a hole in solid wood. Then, using the base of a plastic bottle as shown opposite, see how you can bore a tunnel in wet sand.

Sand

Cut out segments from bottom of plastic bottle. Angle segments as shown

Hydraulic pistons

The TBM cutting head is pushed hard against the rockface using pistons like those in a bicycle pump. Unlike a bicycle pump, though, which is filled with air, the TBM pistons are filled with liquid. But the effect is the same, as you can try for yourself. Put a paper bag under a pile of books. Then blow air into the bag. Because fluids are hard to compress, they can be used to transfer pressure from, say, your lungs to the books — or from a piston ram to the TBM cutting head!

Hydraulic pistons on the TBM

Books

Paper bag

Hydraulic fluid

Piston

TUNNELS WORLDWIDE

Tunnels are being used increasingly in road and rail transport, for several reasons. They can follow the most direct route between two places. They can be used in any weather conditions. They can be built without disrupting existing communications. And they do not disturb the scenery or environment too much.

Tunnels are some of the biggest structures that engineers have ever built. Some that run under water, such as the Chesapeake Bay Tunnel in the USA, are built by sinking giant tubes onto the sea bed. The tubes are floated into position, their sides are filled with concrete, and then they are lowered into a pre-dug trench. The tubes are joined together and the water is pumped out. Tunnels that take vehicle-carrying trains, like Eurotunnel, already exist in many regions. One example is the Simplon Tunnel, which is not under the sea bed – but through the Alps linking Switzerland and Italy.

NAME	COUNTRY (REGION)	LENGTH	TYPE
West Delaware	USA (New York City)	170 kms	Water supply
Seikan	Japan (Honshu to Hokkaido)	54 kms	Undersea rail
Oshimizu	Japan (near Tokyo)	22 kms	Rail
Simplon	Switzerland-Italy	19.8 kms	Rail
Moscow Metro	USSR	31 kms	Metro railway
St Gottard	Switzerland (Goschenen-Airolo)	16.5 kms	Road
Orange-Fish Rivers	South Africa	83 kms	Irrigation
Chesapeake Bay	USA (Virginia)	28.4 kms	Road bridges and tunnel
Rove	France (Marseilles to Rhone)	7.3 kms	Canal
Majes	Peru	98 kms	Hydroelectricity
(When completed in 1993)			
Channel Tunnel	Britain-France	50 kms	Undersea rail

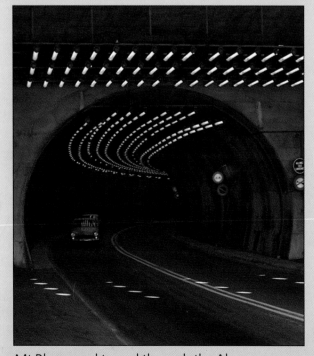

Mt Blanc road tunnel through the Alps

Seikan – the longest rail tunnel in the world

GLOSSARY

Access shaft Tunnel or passageway through which people can enter a site.

Concrete A mixture of cement, fine aggregate (sand), coarse aggregate (gravel or small stones) and water, that sets hard. The setting is a chemical reaction, not a drying-out, so it happens even under water.

Conveyor An endless moving belt that carries objects from one place to another.

Cutting head The boring tool of a Tunnel Boring Machine (TBM). It scrapes, picks and grinds away at the rockface.

Deck A floor or platform suspended from a bridge or built across the base of a ship, tunnel or similar construction.

Elevator A "lift", a small room that travels up and down in a shaft and transports people and goods.

Foundations The base of a building, that transmits its weight safely into the surrounding subsoil and rock and stops it sinking or leaning.

Geology The science of the nature of soils and rocks and, in engineering, how these affect the construction and stability of buildings.

Grout A mixture of cement, water and fine sand that sets hard and is waterproof when dry. It is used to fill cracks and joints in concrete segments.

Hydraulic Worked by fluid under pressure.

Ram A machine that repeatedly drops or pushes a heavy weight onto or into something, or that uses pressure to force something to move forwards.

Reinforced concrete Concrete that sets around metal rods, girders or meshes, to give it greater strength.

Services Electricity, water, drainage, gas and other supplies.

Shuttle A regular to-and-fro service between two terminals (rail, sea, air, etc.)

Spoil Loose rock, earth, sand and mud, removed from an excavation or tunnel-boring site.

Steel Iron from a blast furnace that has had nearly all the carbon removed (down to 1.7 per cent or less) and small quantities of other substances added. There are many types of steel, made hard and tough for various specialized applications.

Surveying The accurate measuring and plotting on a map of the geographical and geological features of a location.

Terminal A main arrival and departure point for train, sea or air passengers.

Through-services Transport system that operates on the same routes as shuttle services but does not operate between the terminals.

Ventilation Some combination of warming, cooling, drying and moistening (humidifying) the air in a building or structure, to make it pleasant for people and suitable for delicate machinery.

INDEX

Photographic Credits:
Cover and all pages to 24 left: Q.A. Photos Ltd; pages 24 right and 25 middle: Channel Tunnel Group Ltd.; page 25 top and all pages to 30: Q.A. Photos Ltd; page 30 left: Rex Features; page 30 right: Spectrum Colour Library

PRINTED IN BELGIUM BY

INTERNATIONAL BOOK PRODUCTION